MW01134829

# ZOE'S TREE

Caro Rodriguez

Illustrated by
Kateryna Parfyrieva

**H**alo
PUBLISHING
INTERNATIONAL

ISBN: 978-1-63765-224-4

Halo Publishing International, LLC
www.halopublishing.com

Printed and bound in the United States of America

To the women in my life: my mom Janneth, my grandmothers Iraida Teresa and Maria Victoria, and my nieces Emma Sofia and Valeria Valentina.

— Caro

This is the story of a little girl, named Zoe, who dreamed of a beautiful, tall tree.

Every time she felt happy, her tree would blossom with beautiful pink flowers.

Her tree glowed brightly as the sun kissed its petals and warmly hugged its branches.

Every time she felt lonely, she would cry under her tree.

As the tears ran down her rosy cheeks, the delicate flowers would start to fall from its branches, gently landing on her lap.

Zoe would then look around her and realize she was not alone.

Every time she felt angry, she would scream at her tree so loud that her voice was confused with the roaring thunders.

Her tree started to look different and its glow faded under the gloomy sky.

Zoe felt she was growing away from her tree every time she blinked... Until she completely lost sight of it.

She was scared she might have lost it forever.

She waited eagerly to go to bed every night, with the hopes of falling asleep and dreaming of her beloved, humble tree.

But she couldn't.

One day, Zoe went to see her grandma, who was sitting on the porch of her house, peacefully contemplating a piece of paper.

Zoe rushed towards her lap and asked, "Grandma? how do trees grow strong enough to survive a storm?"

"Sweetheart, trees don't grow overnight," said Grandma as she started to fold the piece of paper. "They grow with patience!"

"How?" asked Zoe with her eyes wide open. Her thin, brown eyebrows raised in suspense as she waited for her grandma to reveal the secret of trees.

"For trees to grow strong, their seeds should be planted in nourishing soil. You must water them every day to make sure they can start slowly sprouting their branches."

"Is that all?" asked Zoe.

"No, sweetheart," replied Grandma. "That's just the beginning!"

Grandma continued folding the piece of paper as she explained:

"You must protect your tree from the moment it's just a little branch. It might not be strong enough to survive on its own.

People might get distracted and step on its little branches without noticing. If this happens often, your little tree won't be able to grow past the surface of the soil.

You must build a little fence around your tree so that others can be more careful! Only those who are willing to take care of your tree will be allowed to walk past your fence and help you water it."

"At times, trees must learn to adapt to harsh environments.

Long droughts, heavy rains, and whirling winds...

They can appear suddenly, without warning, and blow everything away!" said Grandma.

Zoe's curious face turned into worry.

Grandma smiled looking into Zoe's eyes and said:

"As long as its roots are firmly grounded, and its branches are flexible, your tree will have the resilience it needs to withstand anything."

Zoe smiled in relief.

Grandma continued to share her words of wisdom as she kept on folding the paper.

"It's important you give your tree enough space for its roots to grow deep into its life-giving soil, and for its branches to reach unimaginable places."

"With enough nutrients, space, patience, and strength... Oh my darling, your tree will blossom!

No person, no storm, absolutely nothing, will have the power to keep that from happening!"

Zoe's eyes filled with joy as her grandma leaned towards her and put a beautiful paper flower in her hands as she whispered:

"As long as you are there for your tree, your tree will always be there for you!"

"To give you the most beautiful flowers and brighten up your saddest days,

to give you the shade you
need to escape the heat
and take a break,

to let you swing on its
branches every time
you want to play,

and to make you feel at ease
with the most melodious birds."

"One day, sweetie, your beautiful, flowered tree will be very tall and strong.

When that happens, you must build a tree house in it!

A happy place where you can work and play...

Where no fences are needed...

Where you can teach others to protect their trees with the same love and patience you protected yours," explained Grandma.

From that day on, Zoe looked at the paper flower as her most precious treasure and kept this memory in her heart forever and ever.

Printed in the USA
CPSIA information can be obtained
at www.ICGtesting.com
LVHW061458290124
770238LV00008B/244